Deck the Halls

LEARN WREATH DESIGN

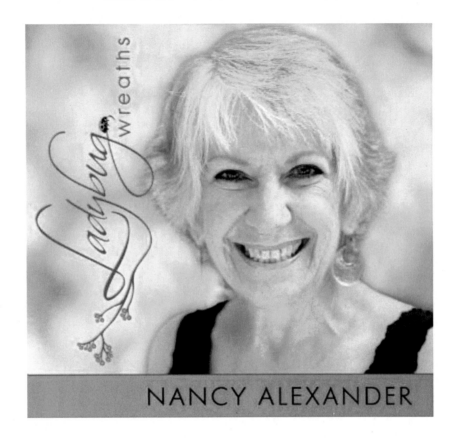

NANCY ALEXANDER

By World-Renowned

Floral Designer – Nancy Alexander

Want to Watch a Free Wreath Tip Video from Nancy?

Go To: www.LadybugWreaths.com/sg

Publisher's Disclaimer

No part of this book may be duplicated, stored in an information retrieval system, or sent in any form or by any available resource, electronic, mechanical, photographic reproduction, recorded material, scanning, optically, either digital or analog or otherwise, except as permitted under Section 107 or 108 of the 1976 United States Copyright Act, without the prior written permission of the Publisher or Author.

Requests to the Author or Publisher for permission should be addressed to:
Ladybug Wreaths
203 Regent Road
Anderson, SC 29621

Limit of Liability/Disclaimer of Warranty: While the publisher and the author have used their best abilities in assembling this book, they make no representations or warranties with respect to the exactness or wholeness of the contents of this book and particularly reject any implied warranties of marketability or appropriateness for a particular purpose. No warranty may be developed or continued by sales representatives or written sales materials.

The information and methods contained herein may not be useful for your circumstances. The reader should confer with a professional where suitable. Neither the publisher nor the author shall be responsible for any loss of profit or any other commercial injuries, including but not limited to special, incidental, significant, or other damages.

If you would like to begin receiving our popular and Free newsletter with valuable information, visit: http://www.LadybugWreaths.com. We would love to add you to our subscriber list.

Please email nancy@LadybugWreaths.com to report illegal distribution.

As of the writing of this book, all information is current. Please note that over time, this type of information may change – especially when writing and picturing seasonal items.

CONTENTS

ABOUT THE AUTHOR

Nancy Alexander is a wife, mother, Mimi, sister, best friend, and child of God.

As a Dreamer, Artisan, Teacher, Public Speaker, Coach and Internet Entrepreneur, it didn't take long for her to become known as a world-renowned Floral and Interior Designer.

After over 30 years of running her own businesses, she now sells popular floral designs, as well as her how-to, instructional DVDs and downloadable videos and supplies to make these wreaths.

But, that's not all! Nancy is a published author offering several popular Books, Kindle Books, and eBooks. Her life story, is almost finished, and will soon be published.

Nancy is blessed to know, work, and partner with many of the most talented "Internet Entrepreneurs" in the business.

Nancy **LOVES** her students, as she shares in their joy and excitement with every accomplishment!

 "Nancy's dreams of making YOUR dreams come true by equipping and teaching YOU to become a success!" You'll quite often hear Nancy's encouraging words saying "You Can Do It!...I Know YOU Can!"

In the last 10 years well over 3,000 wreaths have been shipped to happy customers all over the world. She has sold thousands of videos and books which teach her customers how to design and sell their own floral creations!

Nancy, and her best friend and partner, Linda Joseph, offer private and group coaching. This one-on-one or group coaching has made a huge difference in many lives. You can find more information about these coaching venues on their latest website: **www.PassionIntoProfits.com**

Their coaching/membership site, **www.BestOfNancy.com** encourages and trains women to develop their "artisan" skills as they learn to sell and promote crafts and products online through many venues.

Another Ladybug Wreath's site, **www.LadybugCertified.com** provides the exact same supplies Nancy uses in all her wreaths. Available from Amazon, shipping is FREE with Amazon Prime. Benefits are...no Sales Tax ID is required; no case quantities; no minimums; and super-fast shipping.

Group & Private (VIP) workshops offered in her home studio are such fun. After experiencing a "Studio Day" with Nancy, each lady departs with a gorgeous wreath and an easel. They possess the tools to start a budding business or to make gorgeous wreaths as a hobby.

Nancy says: "I am thrilled to know these ladies are leaving with confidence and knowledge to set up online and offline businesses to sell their beautiful creations. But, most importantly, I am also filled with JOY as they leave with hugs, laughter, and lots of smiles."

Nancy has been encouraged, and coached by her mentor and dear friend, Jim Cockrum. Nancy admires Jim and calls him one of the most ethical Internet Marketers around, and all the while Jim says *"Nancy has inspired me* more than I could *ever* inspire her." As a matter of fact, Jim has written about Nancy in his newly published book; **"FREE Marketing 101"**. This book is **the number one** book on Internet Marketing in the world!

Nancy is inundated with emails and calls from her faithful followers who want and need her help. You see, Nancy has been fighting a painful battle with Fibromyalgia and Celiac Disease after becoming severely ill at twenty-eight years of age. Thanks to her husband, Steve, amazing doctors and God's leading; she is enjoying a new life!

Nancy has a heart-felt yearning to help others regain their health, & experience positive changes as she has. She desires for each of you to find joy, health, and happiness through God's leading and through your own successful business. This has turned into quite a ministry for Nancy and Steve.

INTRODUCTION

**Welcome and Congratulations on your purchase of
"Deck The Halls" Wreath Instructional Book!**

Wreath making can become one of the easiest and most delightful hobbies you will ever undertake. I taught myself how to make a wreath many, many years ago during a difficult time in my life. I was struggling to feel normal while experiencing chronic pain, so wreath making became an outlet of self-expression and creativity. I first sold my wreaths at craft shows, and after finding success there, I purchased a local shop called The Straw Basket. This purchase was a highlight in my life, allowing me to develop my own style in floral design. The business grew, taking me down several avenues, which eventually led me to eBay. I didn't stop there! I now sell wreaths to faithful customers all over the world, while other parts of my business continue to grow by leaps and bounds.

For many years I have received requests from friends, customers, and new acquaintances alike wanting to learn my style in designing one-of-a-kind wreaths. Customers and friends in my hometown tell me when they visit a home or doctor's office in town; they always recognize my wreaths and my style immediately. Well, this book is geared to instruct, but most of all to help you develop your own style, which has been and will always be my goal!

I have poured hours of labor and creativity into "Deck The Halls" so that you can learn the basics -- each step in building (and yes, it is a building process) your own wreath. **I will be sharing with you some of my tips and secrets for making gorgeous wreaths.** I encourage you to follow along closely and then add your own creative touch.

These quality tips and secrets will help you make your very own wreath that can withstand the weather, birds looking for a place to nest, and the occasional fall from your door. If you begin each wreath or design in the right way by tightly securing each stem, bloom, bird, birdhouse, nest, etc., then your wreath will hold up for many, many years. Sun damage, which, unfortunately, is inevitable, may occur, even with quality materials.

You will also learn how to make your wreath "wild & woodsy", "light & airy", or very full and formal.

These phrases have described my personal style, but in the long run, and with lots of practice, you will eventually start to see your own style developing. This style will be exclusive to you, your likes and dislikes, and will reflect the unique and special person that you are. _I can guarantee that it will be absolutely beautiful!!_

Deck The Halls also includes a list of suggested supplies, in addition to a list of the particular items I used for the wreath on the cover. Please go to your local craft/floral store to purchase the stems that best suit your style and taste, or visit my supplies store: **www.LadybugCertified.com**. Always remember, available supplies change from year to year. You may not be able to purchase exactly what I used here. Just find something as close as you can.

I offer several books as well as instructional DVDs and digital videos and wreath design. You can learn more in the **Resource Appendix**.

ITEMS YOU WILL NEED

Wreath Making Tools

- **Glue gun and glue sticks***
- **Wire cutters***
- **Floral tape**
- **Picks**
- **Pipe Cleaners**
- **Easel (optional)***

  ***NOTE**: I use a custom made easel which you can purchase here as well as other tools: http://ladybugwreaths.com/doorwreaths/product/wreath-making-supplies/

Supplies for the Deck the Halls Wreath

(Supplies can be found Your Local Craft Store or wholesale supplier.)

- **Twenty-Four Inch Green Christmas Wreath**
- **Roll of #40, Wired, Stiff Ribbon...Sparkly & shiny**
- **Green ficus stem**
- **Ivy bunch**
- **Green grasses**
- **Seven or eight pieces of Iced or sugared fruit**
- **Red filler – mine was red leafy filler**
- **Holly berry bush – lighter green leaves w/red berries**
- **Airy Christmas filler – with small cones if possible**
- **A red bird, and maybe a nest (I didn't use one here)**

Use your personal style to decide the colors and exact stems you purchase. (You don't have to use my exact elements.) Just purchase something similar so the finished wreath will have the same look as mine. It can even be in different colors!

MAKING YOUR WREATH

CHAPTER 1 – PREPARE YOUR WREATH

Place the green Christmas wreath on your easel or door until it hangs evenly to find a top and a bottom. If you would like to create a more "wild and woodsy" look, even in a green Christmas wreath, you can add loops and curls of honeysuckle vine just like I use in my everyday "wild birch" wreaths.

Begin by picking up one of the green, wired extensions or stems (pipe cleaners).

Working from the back of your wreath, attach the chenille stem to the metal wire base of the wreath and twist it creating a loop at the top to hang your Christmas Wreath.

Do you know how to fluff a wreath?

Well, that part is next, and that is what I am doing in the following picture.

I reach right into the center of the wreath, straightening out each wired green extension pulling it so it is straight, with no bend in it. I don't want the stems, or extensions, pointing in the same direction, so I pull them straightly out and then point them around the wreath as it is lying flat on my work counter. You can see in the picture below how they are pointing in various directions.

Here you can see that I am reaching way into the wreath making sure no stems are lying flat. I really want to make sure each and every one of them is sticking out from the main base of this thick green wreath.

When finished, there should be some pointing toward the middle, and some pointing toward the outside of your wreath.

Through the years of owning a retail store and selling Christmas wreaths, every member of my family has learned the art of wreath fluffing.

I even taught my daughters-in-law, Sara and Stephanie, how to perfectly fluff a wreath. My boys try to pretend that they don't remember how to do it in an effort to avoid helping during the holidays, but I know they can still do it.

Start with one section and work your way around the wreath. Pull each stem away from the wreath base so that they are no longer lying flat. Fluff the wreath in a half circle design with some stems pointing toward the inside, some toward the outside, and some straight out. The last thing you want is a wreath where all of the stems are pointing straight out.

Above is a picture of a perfectly fluffed wreath. You'll see that some stems point into the center of the wreath, and some point to the outside, and some are spread throughout the center. Beautiful! It is important to spend the extra time fluffing your wreath in the beginning because it makes such a difference in the finished product.

After spending the short time it takes to fluff your wreath, we are ready to have some fun!

The next chapter is the BEST part as far as I'm concerned!

I love making bows; single, double and triple ribbon bows, with many loops and curls, and so will you after a little practice, and experience.

Then, we'll be having lots more fun – and it's really easy! We'll add flower stems, fillers, and fruit into this Christmas wreath that will be a show stopper at your home!

When working with a green Christmas base, you'll see how really easy it is. You have all the wired green extensions that you can wrap around ribbon loops, stems, and anything else you are adding to your wreath. Actually, green Christmas wreaths (I believe) are the easiest ones to make!

But, I don't just anchor everything in that way – I also put lots of hot glue which really sticks well to the green wreaths.

CHAPTER 2 – READY TO MAKE A BOW?

Put your fluffed wreath aside and pick up your ribbon. We're going to make a bow!!! Yes, "You are", and you _will_ be able to do it! Don't you LOVE this ribbon with its glittering look and glistening threads?

I always recommend using a wired ribbon. It is much easier to learn on and it holds its shape much better. If it is your first bow, please don't buy a ribbon that is not wired, and also, please do not buy a ribbon that is really thick – such as red velvet.

I'll go through the following pictures quickly; step-by-step so you can see the process. Then I'll make the same bow again as I write in detailed descriptions exactly what I'm doing.

I would really like for you to learn on a ribbon that is wired, and a little stiff, but still easy to hold.

It will take you a little while to build up the strength in your hands to hold onto the loops and streamers tightly until the bow is finished.

I will be using the most popular size used at Christmas – a #40, which is 2 ½ inches wide. Begin by measuring out 30 inches of ribbon for your first streamer (leaving it hanging down against you). Pinch the ribbon together at this point as I am doing in the picture to above.

Now, if you have any problems following my written instructions as you are learning to make your first bow, I have several bow-making videos on my YouTube channel that you can watch.

It is: www.YouTube.com/LadybugWreaths

First, start with a streamer which is about 30 inches long. The streamer should be pointed toward your body (and the rest of the ribbon pointed away from your body) as you begin. Pinch the ribbon together as you point it away from your body, and then back underneath the first pinch. THIS IS YOUR FIRST LOOP!

Pinch and twist it so that the pattern of the ribbon stays on the top as you bring the loop toward your body, and back underneath. THIS IS YOUR SECOND LOOP!

These first two loops should look like a BOW TIE, and be the exact same size – you can see this in the picture above. If you mash them flat, each should measure approximately 7 inches (unless you need a much smaller, or larger bow, this is the normal size). When making my bows I put my loops in layers, working down (or underneath) as I go.

Now, the second layer is an X. As I am making the four loops of the X, I make all four of them about an inch and a half longer than the loops of the first bowtie.

Your next loop (the first of the X) will be pulled away from your body, and then looped back underneath.

I am pinching and twisting the ribbon each time it is in the center of the bow. The second loop of the X will go toward you, then back under toward the center of the bow again.

I know this sounds confusing... but go to my YouTube page and watch me making a wreath like this, and it will all begin to make sense. (http://www.youtube.com/ladybugwreaths)

Do this again 2 more times so that you have the four loops of the X. Each one is pointing outward, and not toward the inside of the bow.

Below is a picture of my bow so far. How does yours look? As you can see, we are shaping the bow as we go. You can see the bowtie, as well as the X. When you are finished, your bow will be the perfect shape with only a slight tug here and there.

Just look at these beautiful loops...

This is why I stress the importance of purchasing wired ribbon. Unwired ribbon creates a bow that is "floppy" and doesn't always hold its shape. But ours looks perfect!

For smaller projects, I could really stop right here, but I am making a larger Christmas Wreath today, so we'll keep on adding loops. And...if you want to make a topper for your tree, you use these exact same steps as above, making more and more loops with each set getting larger as you go! SO SIMPLE!!

With the first "bowtie" and "X" finished, let's add more to the bow! Under the four loops that resemble an "X", make another two loops that look like another "bowtie". You can see in the picture above the three layers of "bowtie", "X", and then "bowtie". Each layer is about an inch to two inches longer than the last layer we made.

NOTE: Always remember that you are working away from your body – pointing down toward the floor when making your bow. And, as you make each set such as the bowtie, and the X, each section needs to be about an inch and a half longer than the section above it.

Now, let's make our final loop. This loop comes out the top of the bow giving it that finished look. Begin by twisting the ribbon and bringing it up and over and back down with the streamer coming out the left side of the bow creating the loop at the top of your bow. Twist the ribbon again as it curls down on the left side of your bow to create your second streamer.

We're almost finished!

Here is a picture of the almost completed bow, with just a few more steps to go. We're going to tie it with a pipe cleaner (a chenille stem) to secure it, and then we'll run our fingers down each wired edge of the bow streamers to make your loops curl slightly.

Personally, I love to have my streamers curling sort of wild, but you can't do this unless you purchase wired, semi stiff ribbon to work with.

Because we are using wired ribbon, there is very little "fluffing" to do. Learning to make a bow is a wonderful skill that you can use over and over! And it is much easier than most people think!

It is a good idea to buy some wired #40 ribbon that is on sale, or at a good price, and begin practicing making your bows.

Then, take the bow apart – iron it if necessary – and make another! The only way you'll become an expert in bow making is to practice, practice, and more practice!

The more you play at making beautiful bows, and the more bows you make, the easier it will become and the stronger your hands will be for holding the ribbon.

Speaking of hands... at first, your hands will hurt when making a bow. It really gets me in my right thumb, and around my wrist each year as we switch over to the Christmas season. Don't worry, your hand will get stronger and stronger as you go!

Remember... I KNOW you can do it! ☺

CHAPTER 3 – YOU DID IT! A BEAUTIFUL BOW

While you are holding the bow very tightly with your fingers, pick up a green or red pipe cleaner. We are going to use it to secure the loops tightly together.

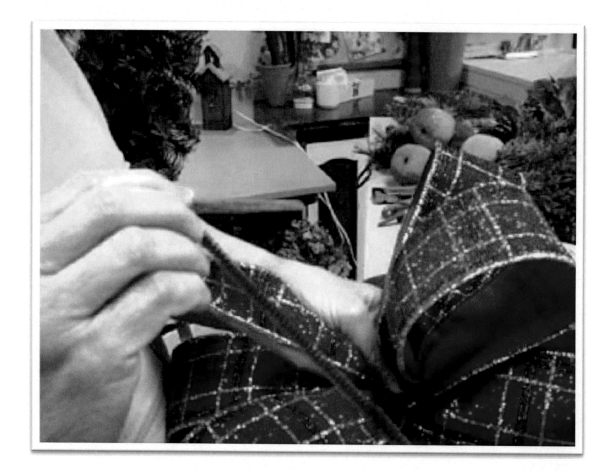

I prefer to always use a pipe cleaner when you are securing my bows. Because I have found that I tend to cut my fingers with wire when trying to tie a bow tightly.

Compared to wire, they are much easier to work with and won't cut your fingers. And that's a very good thing!

Quick note:

If your ribbon is very thick or if you have made a large bow – say for a tree topper – it's best to double your pipe cleaner just in case. You certainly don't want it to break. And, I have to admit that I have broken my share of pipe cleaners!

Fold the pipe cleaner in half and place it over the spot where you are pinching all of the loops together. You'll thread it through your fingers so that you don't have to let go of your bow.

Continue to hold the loops very tightly. Your loops will slide out the side of your hand if you don't keep a tight hold on them!

Pull the green pipe cleaner completely around all of the ribbon and pull it as tightly as you possibly can. Be sure to twist the pipe cleaner several times so that it securely holds all of the ribbon together.

The secret of a really good bow that will stay in place and hold its shape is how securely you tie it after it has been made. So, I would practice this step also… making it very sturdy.

Now, cut the ends of both streamers into a "V", just like I have done in the photo above. Set your completed bow aside for now because there is something else we need to take care of before securing out pretty bow!

Before we insert our bow, I want to add a piece of ribbon to the wreath that I know will give it that extra special touch!

CHAPTER 4 – SECURE YOUR BOW TIGHTLY

In this picture you can see that I am holding up a separate piece of ribbon on the upper left side of the wreath. Measure out 1-¼ yards of ribbon from your spool and cut it off. Cut a "V" on both ends of the streamers.

Notice in this picture how I am twisting 2 of the green extensions of my wreath tightly around the piece of ribbon I just added. That is also where the bow will be attached. Watch, and you'll see what I am doing.

Ribbons are very easy to secure in green Christmas wreaths. Everyone has their own preference as to where she would like her bow.

You can place the ribbon on either side of the wreath; just decide where you would like for your bow to rest and place the ribbon there.

I just happen to like mine in the upper left... just a little off center. This makes it easier for me to place my streamers when I start running them through the wreath as I tuck, and curl, and twist them in.

Once secure, pull the ribbon towards you so that it isn't lying flat on the wreath.

When you tie your bow into our wreath you will use the pipe cleaner you used to secure the bow. You will secure it right into the same spot where you twisted in the extra piece of ribbon. This creates the look of four streamers instead of two.

In the following picture you can see the strip of ribbon after I have twisted two of the wired extensions of the green Christmas wreath around it.

I am going to leave it that way right now, but don't worry... we'll get back to it after adding our bow, and we'll have it looking great in absolutely no time!

I want you to tie the bow right in the middle of the streamers that we have just secured – exactly in the same place it was tied it.

Now, let's thread the pipe cleaner through the wreath making sure you tie it to one or two of the sturdy wires which hold your wreath together. Remember? This is the same way we tied our pipe cleaner on to make a loop for hanging. Be sure to pull it tightly.

I would like for you to tie your bow in so tightly that it will not move at all when you twist and pull your loops around where you might like them to go.

If they do move as you are working with them, one of two things might be wrong. First, you may not have tied your bow tightly enough when you made it originally.

Secondly, you may not have tied it tightly enough to your wreath with your pipe cleaner. When tying your wreath onto the wreath make sure the pipe cleaners or wire catch hold of one of the metal circular rings that your wreath is made of.

CHAPTER 5 – STREAMER TIPS AND SECRETS

Now that the bow is securely placed in your wreath, let's work with our streamers to give them an extra special touch. Notice how I am running my hand down the wired edge of the ribbon.

That makes it curl slightly – you know – sort of like curling ribbon you would use for Birthday packages.

It's the little details like curling the ribbon that will make your wreath so unique and elegant, don't you think?

After curling the streamer, tuck it into the wreath. Don't pull it too tightly; you want to maintain the "loose-flowing" feel of the ribbon. Use the green wired stems of the wreath to tie around the ribbon and hold it tightly.

Here you can see how I am pinching each streamer after I have curled it with my hands. Do this with all four of the streamers.

The two that came out of the bow are secured furthest down toward the bottom of the wreath. I am tucking in the other two streamers on each side of the bow so that they wrap around the wreath.

Don't forget to secure the ribbon by wrapping the green stems of the wreath around it tightly. Do you know? This is why I LOVE making Christmas wreaths!

You already have your greenery underneath before you start designing. You have wired extensions coming out from the wreath to help twist and hold everything that you add.

I don't let this keep me from using glue, because I definitely always use glue to put everything in even more securely.

Doesn't this look beautiful so far. It looks fabulous already! We could stop right here and have a perfectly lovely Christmas wreath, but I think we should keep going! I want to show you what we can really do!

We have wonderful stems of greenery, fruit and filler still left to add! Before I get ahead of myself, (I am just really excited about this wreath!), let's do a couple of extra things to make sure our bow doesn't go anywhere!

Next, we're going to work on all of the outside loops of our bow. It will look much prettier if we spread the loops out. Do you know how I make sure they stay in place? Well… I'll tell you… it is SO easy!

I use the green extensions from the wreath and wrap a few of them around the backs loops of my bow.

This holds them securely in place, so that they never come loose! I always make sure to do this part before adding the rest of my flowers, ornaments, greens, and whatever else I may be adding to my Christmas Wreaths!

CHAPTER 6 – WISPY GREENERY MAKES A DIFFERENCE

Now let's get to the fun and exciting details I was telling you about! I have this wonderful greenery that I love to add to all of my Christmas wreaths. It doesn't matter if the greenery you bought looks like mine or not, it will add so much to the wreath! We never want our wreaths to keep the stiff, tight appearance that they have straight from the manufacturer.

It is really a good idea if you can find some lighter colored greens than the color of your green wreath.

It just gives it a great contrast. I am a BIG fan of using contrasting shades of green in every single wreath that I design.

If you are using airy green garlands such as these, just cut them into small pieces, making them go a long way. Use picks on them if necessary, because one end – if stuck way inside the wreath – will not show at all anyway.

Begin by cutting your airy green garlands. You can use a garland like I am or greenery stems, or even picks.

Once these items go on sale at your local hobby/craft store, they will be reduced every few weeks, so you can save money by watching your ads and buying at the right time.

Once your airy greenery has been cut up, you can start adding it to your wreath.   Tuck it throughout making sure that it radiates out from you wreath some.

With this greenery, we can start getting that "Wild & Woodsy" look that everyone loves so much. This green stem is also a lighter green. Anytime you can add light green, or lime green to your other greens... it really makes the colors pop.

Notice how I do not stick it in very closely. I like to leave it flowing out of the wreath, filling my bow, in order to obtain a really airy and full look.

Continue adding the pieces around your entire wreath. All of these stems are added by applying hot glue on the ends of each stem. These stick in to the green wreaths very easily and the glue grabs hold to the wreath stems around it very nicely.

I especially like how this airy greenery looks next to my bow. Our bows are different than most – have you noticed?

We at Ladybug Wreaths like to tuck everything we can into them including fruit and greenery! By doing this, we are making sure that the bow really blends into the wreath as it becomes an element of this design rather than standing out like a colored ball!

By filling in the spaces of the bow with other items, the bow will blend into the wreath and not stand out too much.

I keep looking out my window and wishing that the outdoor weather reflected the wonderful Christmas feeling that I'm experiencing making this wreath! (But instead it's almost 100 degrees outside!) ☺

Here is a picture of my wreath so far. How does yours look?

Are you starting to get excited? We still have a ways to go, but it is looking so pretty already!

CHAPTER 7 – LEAFY EUCALYPTUS ADDS TEXTURE

Now I'm going to add another kind of greenery to my Christmas wreath. These are small leafy eucalyptus bushes.

Cut each bush into individual stems. And place them around your wreath by applying hot glue down the stem.

One of the great things about Christmas wreaths is that they look absolutely wonderful when you add everyday greens to them as well as Christmas greens.

I always like to use a large mix of greens. The more, the better, as far as I'm concerned. And they don't have to be all Christmas greens either. A mix of everyday greens looks great too. The more contrasting greens you have the more character your wreath will have.

You're probably wondering why I haven't talked about picks yet. That's because I didn't use a single pick on the greenery in this entire wreath! Instead, I used them on the fruit only. Let me tell you why.

Floral picks are always used in my wild birch wreaths to secure stems of all sizes. When used properly, making sure the wire is tightly wrapped around the pick and stem; floral picks are the perfect support to push your stems into a wild birch wreath.

A pick anchors a stem into the wreath. So you're probably wondering why I didn't use them for my greens in this wreath, aren't you? The difference is in the wreaths. Green Christmas wreaths have stems that "grab" hot glue when it touches them. Wild birch wreaths do not.

In the previous picture, you can see where I added some of the leafy eucalyptus stems. I spread the hot glue along the stem of the green, and I even put some on the bottom leaves of the eucalyptus.

The glue "grabs" the green stems of the wreath and holds on tightly. You still want to make sure that all of your stems are properly anchored in the wreath. I always build my wreaths to withstand the regular wear and tear of life.

CHAPTER 8 – NEED MORE COLOR WITH RED FILLERS

These leafy stems will add so much to our wreath! Now that we have added our leafy green stems, let's move onto our delightfully cheerful red leafy stems. Look at the rich color!

These leafy stems will add so much to our wreath! These bushes are hard to find, but I love using them in all of my Christmas wreaths!

These stems are thick and full of color; they add great depth to the design. You can cut them as thick or thin as you prefer and can place them anywhere you like as long as you can anchor them securely into the wreath.

After cutting up the red leafy bush into individual stems, let's add them to our wreath!

I'm going to place a stem in the bottom of my wreath. I like the way it drapes down and mimics the movement of the streamer beside it. I think we should add another red stem beside this one.

So what do you think of the wreath so far?

As you can see, I added the red leafy filler on the sides of the wreath as well as the top and bottom.

The stems on the sides and bottom drape down, while the stems on the stop of the wreath stand up straight giving it height.

Beautiful Wreath So Far...Let's Keep Going!

CHAPTER 9 – WHAT A DIFFERENCE ICED FRUIT MAKES

Let's dive right into the next part of our wreath: fruit! Fruit adds such a wonderful touch to a wreath, especially to a Christmas wreath.

As I mentioned earlier, I was inspired to use fruit in my Christmas wreaths after learning about the Colonial Williamsburg style. This style is rich with history dating back to the beginning years of our nation.

We've added our modern touch, stepping away from the compact and symmetrical wreaths of the past, and using iced fruit instead of real.

We begin by preparing our fruit to fit snuggly and securely into our wreath. Grab a handful of 5 inch picks to have nearby.

Press the pick firmly into the bottom side of each piece of fruit. Cut off 2 inches of the pick so that you are left with about 2 ½ inches sticking out. Do this for all of your fruit. Notice how I did not insert the pick straight into the bottom.

It is important that you do not put the pick straight into the bottom of the fruit, but instead insert it at an angle. This will allow you to place your fruit at varying angles.

Now that we have firmly inserted our picks into the fruit, let's add the hot glue. As you can see in the picture below, I am liberally applying hot glue to the bottom of the fruit and to the stem of the pick. This will allow the glue to "grab" the stems around it for a secure fit.

If you have used a lot of ribbon in your bow as I have done and added streamers, then it isn't necessary to add an abundance of materials like we do in our wild birch wreaths.

I inserted my red apple in the bottom of the wreath near the red leafy filler. Make sure to push the apple all the way in.

The glue that you added to the bottom of the fruit and the pick will "grab" the greens around it so that the fruit won't fall out.

Next, I added the delicious green pear. I just love how real this fruit looks, even with the "icing". I inserted my pear into the top of my bow.

I always put at least one piece of fruit in my bow and then alternate colors as I go around the wreath. This decorating tip is very important because it will add visual interest to the wreath.

All of the different colors of the iced fruit add such wonderful contrast and color! Don't be afraid to mix lime colors and orange into your wreaths. Notice how I added more glue once the orange was inserted.

I don't do this on every one, but this one just didn't feel like it grabbed hold as tightly as I thought it should. This fruit isn't going anywhere!

With an orange and an apple nearby, I think we should add another green pear to the bottom of the wreath. Pay careful attention to the angles that I am using to insert the fruit.

Just like floral stems in a wild birch wreath, we don't want the fruit just simply sit there. We want it to look natural and alive. You do not have to use the exact type of fruit that I did. Just make sure to vary the colors and types as you move around the wreath.

How are things going with your fruit? Are you finding the right places to put them?

The picture above of the wreath shows where I have inserted my five pieces of fruit.

My final piece, a purple pomegranate is situated on the side right corner. I love the contrast of the purple and red, don't you?

I'm going to take a few moments right her to talk about "your" style, and not my style.

In order to help you in your quest to learn to make your own wreaths, I not only need to teach you how, but I need to show you too!

But my main goal is and has always been to teach you the basics, and to find your own style. After you learn the basics, your style will begin shining through when you lease expect it!

That is when the "light bulb" comes on in your head and you realize...you just know...that you "have it"!

You are working on creating something very special and very beautiful from your own imagination – from colors you love – to materials which strike your fancy. You then put these together in such a way that is exclusive only to you! (not Ladybug Wreaths...)

That is when I know I have succeeded in teaching you to make your own wreath! This makes me SO happy!

Your questions and your desires to create and learn were the main reasons I started filming my instructional DVDs. I decided that was truly the best way I could help you. I would dearly LOVE to stand right beside each of you and guide your hands in the beginning of this process! This desire is where "Studio Days With Nancy" were born.

And, I must tell you – these days have been amazing. So many ladies have left my workshop with beautiful wreaths, smiles, and confidence that they can now design many, many more!

I want you to know that it's okay to make a mistake! I make them all the time, but I have learned how to correct them. Believe me, all veteran designers make mistakes in their wreaths just as beginning designers do!

The key is knowing how to keep right on going as you correct each mistake; making it all come together to be a gorgeous, finished product in the end. I have always said that really is the key to being a good designer – no matter what happens while you're making a wreath or an arrangement; it's knowing how to bring it all together in the end that counts!

I have taught so many of you in my home studio how to make beautiful wraths! I am so proud of each and every one of you… and I have NEVER had anyone who left here without a big smile on their face, and a wreath that was not gorgeous.

CHAPTER 10 – DIFFERENT LOOK WITH HOLLY BERRIES

"It's a holly, jolly Christmas...it's the best time of the year...." Oh boy, just thinking about this step puts me in the Christmas spirit.

I always love adding holly bushes to my Christmas wreaths. Check my website www.mysecretvendors.com for my "Secret Supplier List" to find several great vendors who have beautiful holly bushes like the ones I like to use for reasonable prices!

For this particular wreath I chose a holly bush with beautiful light green leaves to accent the darker green in the wreath.

The colors vary from dark green to a cheerful lime green.

Bright red berries adorn the tops adding bursts of color against the greens. So cheerful! The greens in this holly bush show up beautifully beside your darker Christmas greens.

Cut all of your stems off of the bush. Add a long stream of hot glue, to the stem of the holly. You do not need to add a pick to these greens. Remember, the glue will "grab" the greens around it, giving it a secure fit.

Tuck the stems in all around your wreath. Let them come out the front, sides, and around the bow. It is important that your greenery is visible from all angles.

Remember, your wreath will be viewed from multiple angles depending upon where you hang it.

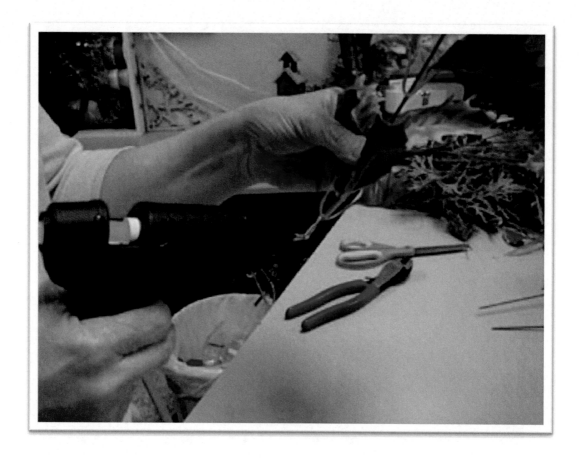

Continue to add glue to each of your holly stems as I am doing in the above picture. You should be able to get lots and lots of stems from the bush. Feel free to add all of them.

As you well know by now, I like for my wreaths to look full. Our goal is to create a perfectly beautiful Christmas wreath that stands out from the ones sold at your local craft/hobby store. And I think that we are on par to do it!

Notice here how I have added lots of my holly in and around my bow. It is important that you add some of each stem, bloom, or filler to the center of your bow. Doing so will make your bow blend into the wreath more.

Now I think I will add some holly to the lower half of my wreath. As you are adding your holly, why don't you take a moment to lay your wreath on a flat surface?

Notice if the stems are radiating out in different angles.

That is the look that we are after. You do not want your stems to all stand straight out. Keep this in mind as you are adding more holly stems.

There is one more place that I want to add a holly stem. On the bottom, under the green pear is the perfect spot, don't you think? How lovely!

Oops! After stepping back and looking at the wreath, I realized that the left side needed another sprig of holly. Ah, now that is much better! Both sides look full and lush!

Notice these lighter green holly berry leaves. Remember before when we were talking about adding lighter greenery right after adding our bow? Well, look at the even lighter shades of these holly leaves, and pay special attention to how they bring this beauty to life.

I know I look a bit concerned in this picture, but I promise you that I am more than pleased with the outcome of our wreath! I just know that you love it as much as I do!

If you like a wild and woodsy wreath with "critters" like me, this is where I might add a bird nest, and a couple of red birds. Any type of critter would be appropriate here, so just gather up the ones you love, put a little glue on the bottoms, and stick them in any spot that makes you smile!

For more wreath ideas and samples go to my website and my wreath galleries:

http://ladybugwreaths.com/doorwreaths/wreaths-for-sale-2/

Summer: http://ladybugwreaths.com/doorwreaths/summer-wreaths/

Baby: http://ladybugwreaths.com/doorwreaths/baby-wreaths-2/

Fall: http://ladybugwreaths.com/doorwreaths/fall-wreaths-2/

Christmas: http://ladybugwreaths.com/doorwreaths/christmas-wreaths-2/

Character: http://ladybugwreaths.com/doorwreaths/character-wreaths-2/

FINISHED WREATH, BY NANCY ALEXANDER

Here is a perfectly delightful picture of our finished wreath! I just love the way it turned out, don't you?

The colors of the fruit contrast nicely with each other, while the delightful mix of greens stands out against the dark Christmas wreath. I also like the way the additional streamers turned out.

By adding a simple piece of ribbon under the bow, we made it look like more ribbon was used than we actually did. The closer that I look at the photo, the more my eyes pick up on the little details.

Do you see how the red holly berries pop out and tie together the red in the wreath! Amazing how such a small detail can become so important, isn't it?

This wreath is sure to wow all of your friends and family! I have a feeling that they will be begging you to make one for them! They certainly would make wonderful Christmas gifts!

APPENDIX- RESOURCE PAGE

LADYBUG NEWSLETTER

Nancy's FREE weekly newsletter contains: decorating ideas; design tips; free 'how to' videos; or special deals. To begin receiving Nancy's newsletter, go to her website: http://www.LadybugWreaths.com . Nancy would LOVE to add you to her mailing list!

INSTRUCTIONAL DVDS & DIGITAL VIDEOS

Nancy offers over 20 instructional videos that show you step by step how to make a particular style of wreath or bow. To view the list of video offerings, go to:

http://ladybugwreaths.com/doorwreaths/product/dvds/
http://ladybugwreaths.com/doorwreaths/download-videos/

WORKSHOPS:

Nancy offers both private and group workshops in her studio in South Carolina. In these workshops you receive personal instruction from Nancy and her assistant on the art of wreath making. You leave with the most beautiful wreath you created and with the knowledge how to make more!

Learn more here:
http://passionintoprofits.com/workshops/

COACHING:

Nancy, along with her friend and partner, Linda Joseph, offer private and group coaching. Our goal is to show you step by step how to sell your wreaths and/or other creations online.

Getting Started Coaching

Many ladies want help turning their creations into a business. "Best of Nancy" is our introductory coaching club. It consists of a forum, video training, monthly updates and bonuses. The forum is a great place to ask questions, meet other like-minded people and find encouragement. The video training covers all the essential elements for selling your creations on the Internet.
To learn more go to:
www.BestofNancy.com

We also offer extended workshops:
www.PassionIntoProfits.com/workshop2/

Purchase My Favorite Supplies From Ladybug Wreaths

Another Ladybug Wreath's site, **www.LadybugCertified.com** provides the exact same supplies Nancy uses in all her wreaths. Available from Amazon, shipping is FREE with Amazon Prime. Benefits are...no Sales Tax ID is required; no case quantities; no minimums; and super-fast shipping.

PURCHASE CUSTOM WREATHS

Nancy continues to create beautiful wreaths that are a treasure for any home. To see her wreaths currently for sale go here:
http://ladybugwreaths.com/doorwreaths/wreaths-for-sale-2/

To order a custom wreath, go here:
http://ladybugwreaths.com/doorwreaths/custom-door-wreaths/

CONNECT WITH NANCY ON FACEBOOK

https://www.facebook.com/nancyladybugwreaths

SUMMARY

How to Make a Gorgeous Wreath

- <u>White Paper</u> - http://www.ladybugwreaths.com/doorwreaths/free-white-papers
- <u>Workshops</u> - http://passionintoprofits.com/workshop1/
- <u>Physical DVDs</u> – http://LadybugCertified.com
- <u>Digital Videos</u> - http://ladybugwreaths.com/doorwreaths/download-videos/

Where to Find the Best Supplies

- <u>Wreath Supplies</u> – http://LadybugCertified.com
- <u>Secret Vendor List</u> – http://MySecretVendors.com

How to Sell Online

- <u>White Paper</u> - http://www.ladybugwreaths.com/doorwreaths/free-white-papers
- Passion Into Profits Coaching – http://PassionIntoProfits.com
  - <u>Best of Nancy Membership</u> – http://BestofNancy.com
  - <u>Workshops</u> - http://passionintoprofits.com/workshop2/

APPENDIX – GETTING STARTED MAKING WREATHS

THREE EASY STEPS TO MAKE YOUR FIRST GORGEOUS WREATH

1. Get Step by Step Instructions

2. Buy Supplies

3. Make a Wreath

STEP 1 - GET STEP BY STEP INSTRUCTIONS

I have produced well over 50 step by step instructional video tutorials and have written several instructional e-Books! The feedback I have received has been overwhelming! Here is just one testimonial:

"Nancy, I have just viewed my copy of your video about the two-foot Christmas tree, and I cannot tell you how much I treasured every moment of it!!! I received it a couple of days ago but put it aside until I had time to savor every minute of it like I was eating a luscious box of chocolates! I love your color choices, and not only did your tree have a wonderful burst of elegant color and glitter, but hanging the greens made the tree have movement as well. You REALLY are a Master Designer and I could watch your video all day.

I shared your website with a professional wedding, floral designer. She was thrilled with your website and had as much of a hard time dragging herself away from it as I did!

Thank you SO much for pursuing your heart's work through your adversities because it is a real inspiration to so many of us too!"
Blessings! ~Carmela~

[NOTE: I have hundreds of testimonials. If you'd like to read a few more, click here. http://ladybugwreaths.com/doorwreaths/how-to-make-wreaths-testimonials/]

You have just purchased the Sunflower Garden e-Book to learn how to make a wreath. How much easier do you think it would be to "watch" me while I do it and explain what I am doing? Yes, it would help a whole lot!

You have two ways to learn from me:

1. Watch one of my many instructional videos

2. Let me teach you in person in my studio!

INSTRUCTIONAL VIDEO

Rather than give you a list of my DVD's to choose from, I want to make this very easy!

To get started:
Just purchase 2 DVDs: "Summer Daze" and "Ribbons and Bows"
[http://ladybugwreaths.com/doorwreaths/product/dvds/dvd-summer-daze/ and
http://ladybugwreaths.com/doorwreaths/product/dvds/how-to-make-a-bow-for-wreaths/]

Summer Daze   **Ribbons & Bows**

All you have to do is watch these two videos! You'll be surprised at how much you learn!

LEARN FROM ME (NANCY) IN PERSON!

Have you ever just wanted to have Nancy stand by your side and show you step by step how to make a wreath?

Well, now you can attend a workshop in her studio!

- **Spend the day with Nancy**
- **Learn in person from Nancy**
- **Immediate feedback from Nancy**

That's right! You can come to my personal shop and learn directly from me! We will start the day at 9:00am in my shop. You will work on your own wreath as I and my assistant lead in the design of a gorgeous wreath.

I provide all the supplies and tools and even an easel. You will be able to ask me any question you want and I will give you immediate feedback on your work. You will complete a 24 inch wreath.

You will learn to ship by boxing and shipping your wreath to your home. You finish the workshop around 4pm with a completed wreath and all the tools, as well as the bonuses.

Learn more about my workshops!
[http://passionintoprofits.com/workshop1/]

STEP 2 – BUY SUPPLIES

You will need some basic supplies for making wreaths.

These wreath making materials include:

- "Wild Birch" wreaths in several sizes made exclusively for LadybugWreaths

- Wreath making easel designed by and made exclusively for LadybugWreaths

- Rolls of freshly harvested honeysuckle vine

- Klein Wire Cutters, my personal favorite

- Sure-bonder Glue Gun or any other hot glue gun

The above is a picture of some of the supplies you will need to get started. You will also need a wreath form (birch or grapevine), honeysuckle vine, and an easel (optional).

CLICK HERE to view wreaths, honeysuckle vine by the roll, and easels on my website:
[http://ladybugwreaths.com/doorwreaths/product/wreath-making-supplies/]
(I have all the details here).

WREATH SUPPLIES

I am so excited to announce that due to an overwhelming demand, we have started to provide my favorite supplies for making wreaths.

These are not just any supplies you can buy at the local craft store.
No Ma'am!
These are the supplies that I, Nancy Alexander, use in my high end wreaths!

Our store will grow, but here are just a few of the items that you will find at:

LadybugCertified.com

STEP 3 – MAKE A WREATH

First I recommend that you spend some time practicing your bow-making skills. Make them over and over again! That is the best way to learn. You can even use the same ribbon, and iron it if necessary in-between bows. The more you practice, the prettier your bows will be.

I would watch "Ribbons & Bows" over several times as you practice your bows. Please don't be discouraged if your first one doesn't turn out as you would like. But after several tries, you'll actually begin to see in your mind where each loop and streamer should be. That's the way it was for me. I did have a hard time with my first several bows.

Then, one day, something just clicked in my mind, and I thought: "WOW, I've Got It!! I can really see the bows as I am making the loops!" And, I did have it! I have been making beautiful bows ever since. And, my bow-making skills are still growing and changing to this day – as I'm sure yours will too.

I PROMISE THAT YOU CAN DO THIS!
I GUARANTEE YOU CAN DO THIS!

Next, you can start working on your wreath. Watch the wreath-making video once all the way through so you can become familiar with the terms, as well as my techniques, tips, and methods. Then you are ready to work along with my video.

Pause the video whenever you need me to stop so you can catch up. Rewind it when necessary. This IS NOT hard. It is SO enjoyable! As you get started, you'll be amazed at what you can accomplish with the correct instructions! Remember again... I know you can do it!

NOTE: Short-cut the process by working with me in person! [http://passionintoprofits.com/workshop1/]

APPENDIX – HOW TO DECORATE A WREATH

STEP 1 - GET STEP BY STEP INSTRUCTIONS

STEP 2 – BUY SUPPLIES

STEP 3 – MAKE A WREATH

Now that you have learned how to make a wreath, you will want to start making wreaths as gifts and for special occasions. Not only will "you" want to start making more wreaths, but friends, neighbors, and even strangers will begin asking you to make wreaths for them. They will like the way your wreaths look so much, that they'll offer to hire you! This is when it is time to start expanding your wreath-making skills; as well as getting many of the questions that begin flying through your head, answered by me.

Beautiful Wreath Made in "Plantation Charm" e-Book

STEP 1 - GET STEP BY STEP INSTRUCTIONS

I have many videos to choose from which cover all seasons and different occasions. Some of these videos come in DVDs, and some are downloadable. More and more are being produced all of the time. These videos include wreath making, table arrangements, table Christmas trees, and tying beautiful bows.

(You can find my DVD selection here: LadybugCertified.com/store)
(You can find my Digital Video selection here: http://ladybugwreaths.com/doorwreaths/download-videos/)

If you aren't sure which to choose next, then I would recommend trying
"Welcome to My Garden"
[http://ladybugwreaths.com/doorwreaths/product/dvds/how-to-make-a-wreath-welcomegarden/]

or "Merry Christmas"
[http://ladybugwreaths.com/doorwreaths/product/dvds/christmas-door-wreath/]

depending on which season you want to focus on, and which style "strikes your fancy".

STEP 2 – BUY SUPPLIES & MATERIALS

You should have the basic supplies for making wreaths. (If not, you can review the list and purchase here.) [http://ladybugwreaths.com/doorwreaths/product/wreath-making-supplies/]

You will definitely want to look over the supplies I use in my wreaths. Go to:
LadybugCertified.com to purchase the quality supplies that I use in my Ladybug Wreaths!

Here is where I do recommend watching the video all the way through at least one time (or more). Some of the wreath-making videos have bows, and some do not – just like some people like bows in their wreaths and some do not. So, decide if you need to purchase ribbon.

When I am purchasing supplies, I usually pick out my ribbon last. It will be much easier to match it to your flowers this way (or at least until you are a little more experienced).

You should buy your materials based on what you see me use in the video you are viewing.

First, you'll notice that I use a large mix of greens.

As you can see in the pictures above, I show you a large mix of greens as I discuss the many types and colors that look great in a wreath! And, I really like using at least three different types of greenery or more such as:

- Short grasses for tight or accent spots on the inside of your wreath. These are great to tuck in and around birds, nests, birdhouses, etc.
- Longer grasses which I use mostly from the outside of the wreath giving it a larger, wilder, and airier look.
- Ivy – I prefer mini leaf with long streamers so it can drape out from the wreath as well as wrapping around some of the honeysuckle vine and wild birch sticks radiating from your wreath.
- Then I always use leafy stems such as wisteria or ficus – and there are many more types of leafy stems. You can get GREAT prices on these if you have purchased "My Secret Vendor List". You can read about it here: "My Secret Vendors". [MySecretVendors.com]
- OR -- You can order the supplies I use here: **LadybugCertified.com**

The pictures above are clips from a video where I show you which flowers I am using. Take note of the types, sizes, and colors of flowers and berries used in the video you have purchased.

- If I am using two or three large flowers, then it will be easier for you to follow along with me if you have two or three large flowers.
- The same applies if I am using medium and small size flowers. Try to purchase stems as close to what I am using as you can. Choose colors that you would like to use.
- Pay special attention to see if I am using a flat flower like a Gerber daisy or a thicker, rounded flower like a hydrangea or a mum. Even this will make a difference when making a wreath for the first time. Later, you'll be able to make substitutions easily.
- And, I also use spiky flowers around the outside of my wreath to bring color out from the center. You can find these in many sizes and colors. Some are called Delphiniums, and then others may just be called flower spikes.
- If using fruit, pick out fruit which you would like to see in your wreath, and the same applies for stems of berries such as crab-apples, or just tiny berry stems.

STEP 3 – MAKE A WREATH

Now you can start making the wreath while you watch the video. Pause the video when you need me to slow down!

ALTERNATIVE – ATTEND A WORKSHOP

I have been asked countless times if I would teach in person. And, I have coached many women as time and health permitted through the years, but not nearly as much or as often as my customers have wanted. So, I will now begin running workshops in my home studio.

We will be offering a limited number of one-day intensive with just "you" and "me". My time will be your time for an entire day! I will teach you how to make any type of wreath that your heart desires!

Next, will be the one-day, Intensive small group workshop. There will be four or five ladies just like yourself. My assistant, Kim, and I will

work one-on-one with each of you as we demonstrate how to make a beautiful wreath. You'll be making yours right along beside us!

Thirdly, is our Premium Intensive TWO day workshop which includes making a wreath as well as learning important business practices, Facebook Page setup, Etsy store setup. You will go home with a beautiful wreath for yourself or we can list it on Etsy, ready to sell! This workshop is designed to REALLY take your wreath-making skills as well as your business to the next level.

Each of these different coaching sessions include, your very own wreath supplies (wire cutters, glue gun, pipe cleaners, picks, floral tape, and green sheet moss), a custom designed "Ladybug Wreaths" easel and a beautiful, finished wreath.

Coaching phone calls with me, as well as our group coaching webinars will also be available if traveling for you is not an option.

If you are interested in these options, schedules, pricing, and other details will be released very soon.   Please make sure that you are on the list by sending a blank email to pipwreath@aweber.com or got to www.LadybugWreaths.com/doorwreaths/free-white-papers.

APPENDIX – HOW TO SELL YOUR WREATHS

Now that you have learned how to make different types of wreaths and have gotten positive feedback from family or friends, you may want to start making some money from your hobby.

Nancy started out years ago selling on eBay and had tremendous success there! It was a great start to her business. However over the years sales started slowing and she looked for other places to sell online.

After a lot of research, Nancy found that Etsy was the best place to sell your wreaths.

NOTE: If you have spent any time on the Internet, you have seen a lot of changes in the Internet and you need to shift your marketing strategies to maximize your online sales.

Etsy has become such a popular venue for handmade items (as well as vintage and other items) that is it not easy to get found and have a lot of sales.

The first step is to start selling on Etsy. You will want to set up your store and list several of your items. Next you need to send interested buyer to your store.

Next we recommend that you create a Facebook page and start building a list of fans who like your creations. This does take time but is a great way to get started.

After you have your Etsy store and a Facebook page, you will want to setup a Pinterest presence. This is a great place to interact with others and to build a following. You can create boards for your different creations.

How to sell online:

1. Etsy (your store)
2. Facebook (your audience)
3. Pinterest (exposure and audience)

BONUS – JUMPSTART YOUR BUSINESS

There is nothing like taking the 'fast track' to starting a business online. I made so many mistakes when I first got started but I plowed through the difficulties even though it took a lot of time and money. However, my income soared once I hired a coach--someone who took me by the hand and guided me through the pitfalls and eliminated my 'trial and errors.'

You can research and figure out how to do this over time. However, there is nothing like taking the 'fast track' to starting a business online. We made so many mistakes when we first got started but we plowed through the difficulties. Even though it took a lot of time and money, we have been able to make a great income.

However, our income soared once we hired a coach--someone who took us by the hand and guided us through the pitfalls and eliminated many 'trial and errors.' Although we are both hard and determined workers, never again will we waste time by trying to build our business without the guidance of a coach or mentor.

We offer two ways to 'jumpstart' your business:

1. Community/Training
2. Workshops

COMMUNITY/TRAINING

<u>Best of Nancy Community</u> (<u>http://BestofNancy.com</u>) – The purpose of this community is to have a place for members to interact and ask question as well as provide the training needed to start selling online.

There are two major benefits to being a part of this awesome group:

- o Forum - The favorite place to hang out for all the members is the forum.
  - You get to know each other and share successes
  - You can share difficulties and get advice and encouragement.
  - You can ask questions when you are stuck

    There are several sections in the forum:
    - Etsy – Member stores and how to use Etsy
    - Facebook – Member pages and how to use Facebook
    - Pinterest – Member Boards and how to use Pinterest
    - YouTube / Websites / Business Strategy/Planning
    - Making Wreaths
    - Boxing Wreaths
    - Shipping Wreaths

- o Training – Video instructions on how to sell on the Internet using:
  - Etsy
  - Facebook
  - Pinterest
  - Website
  - Videos/Checklists/PDFs/Audios
  - Much, much more

WORKSHOPS

(http://passionintoprofits.com/workshop2/)

Our Premium Intensive TWO day workshop enables you to improve your wreath making skills as well as setup your business!

- ○ Day 1 – Nancy will work with you to take your wreath making skills to the next level! You will leave this portion of the training with a beautiful wreath!

  You have all of Nancy's supplies to choose from and you will receive your own wreath making supplies: wire cutters, glue gun, pipe cleaners, picks, floral tape, and green sheet moss.

- Day 2 – Focus on starting your business. We will set up your Etsy store and show you how to create your first listing which will be one of the wreaths you just made in Nancy's shop. Nancy shows you how to take pictures.

  We will then setup you Facebook page and link your Etsy store to your Facebook page. You will learn about business practices, the best way to use social media to build your business and your next steps.

  Your business is started when you leave!

25722967R00064

Made in the USA
Middletown, DE
08 November 2015